Salvatore's Daughter

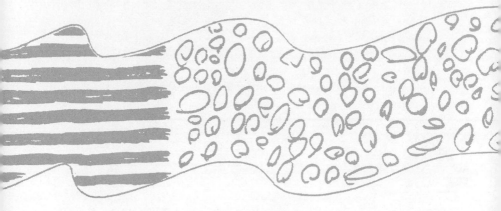

"Maryfrances Wagner writes beautifully and lovingly from her Italian-American heritage, with its emphasis on family and neighborhood, on tradition and continuity, and on humanity's bond with the natural world. In a voice that is sometimes melancholy but never bitter or self-pitying, she moves from a theme of mutability and loss to one of renewal through family and romantic love. These poems consistently engage one with their insight and compassion, their fresh, straightforward language, and their concrete particularity. *Salute* to *Salvatore's Daughter* !"

William Trowbridge
Editor of *The Laurel Review*,
author of *O Paradise*

"These poems of memory have a clarity that prevents them from turning into nostalgia. The poet speaks of her father, Salvatore, his smile, "that had widows bring casseroles." Such attention to language turns these elegies into poems of celebration. Maryfrances Wagner honors us readers, as well, with the details of an authentic life. What we learn to cherish, quite simply, are family, community and the continuity of love."

Robert Stewart
Managing Editor, *New Letters*,
author of *Plumbers*

SALVATORE'S DAUGHTER

Poems by

Maryfrances Wagner

B k M k **Bk Mk** P R E S S

THE UNIVERSITY OF MISSOURI-KANSAS CITY

A C K N O W L E D G M E N T S

Thanks to the following magazines where these poems first appeared.

"Eating an Artichoke," *The Laurel Review* ; "The Woodworker," "The Importance of Kneading," *New Letters* ; "Replay," *Beacon Review* and *Envy's Sting* ; "Arguments," *Green's Magazine* ; "Forsythia," *Nebraska Review* ; "In the Same Place," *Jam Today* ; "What We Become," *Midwest Quarterly* ; "Neighborhood," *Karamu* ; "Slow Losses," "About to Get Up," *Hiram Poetry Review* ; "After Signing Releases," *Rebirth of Artemis* ; "Giant Clown," *Anthology of Missouri Women Writers* ; "Chemotherapy," "Winemaking," "The Occasional Family," "Mask Making," *Kansas City Outloud II* ; "Margaret's Song," *Integrity* ; "The House," "Family," *Caprice* ; "Sisters," *Kansas Quarterly* ; "Salute," *Jam Today* ; "Orange: The Color of Abundance," *Piedmont Literary Review* ; "Snow Angels," *Cape Rock* ; "September 15 in the *Times*," *Poet's Pride* ; "Cafeteria Lady," *Wind* ; "Saying Goodbye to the Children," *Sing Heavenly Muse* ; "In Your Own Way," "Photograph," *Voices of Italian Americana* ; "Mated," "Pilgrims,", "Birds Along the Highway," "Anne's Pond," *Potpourri*.

Copyright © 1995 by Maryfrances Wagner.
Book Design by Thomas Zvi Wilson.
Design production by Michael Annis/Publication Services.

LIBRARY OF CONGRESS
Library of Congress Cataloging-in-Publication Data

Wagner, Maryfrances, 1947-
   Salvatore's daughter : by Maryfrances Wagner.
       p.   cm.
   ISBN 1-886157-00-6
   1. Fathers and daughters--United States--Poetry.   2.   Italian
   American families--Poetry.   3.   Italian Americans--Poetry.
   I. Title.
PS3573.A38647S24   1995
   811'.54--dc20   94-45452
                                                    CIP

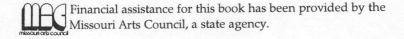 Financial assistance for this book has been provided by the Missouri Arts Council, a state agency.

Bk Mk Press

Dan Jaffe, Director

for my parents
Marguerite and Salvatore Cusumano

with special thanks to Greg,
Margery Lichtor, Louise Andes,
Dr. J. Bisceglia, Dr. Keith Bench
and Judy Theis Roberts
for their support for this book

and in memory of Randy Bates

Salvatore's Daughter

Hands

Of a thousand hands
I would know my father's,
long fingers shaped like oars,
the index scar,
the flat, grooved nails,
hands that fixed the doll's arm,
mended Whisker's ear, checked homework.
Those hands grated romano over Sunday pasta,
curled around glasses of wine
he toasted with at dinner,
or opened to offer the sweetest mulberries,
the ripest figs from his trees.

Once he kept a parsley caterpillar
so I could watch it emerge from its cocoon.
The jar was too small, though;
the wings dried with a crease.
It walked the long ramp of my father's hand,
off balance at takeoff.
It fanned and fanned,
but the crease would not unfold,
the wings could not lift.
My father set it in the grass,
and we watched it walk
the short runway of its life,
a tiny lopsided glider without wind.
My father's hands, like long anchors,
dangled at his sides.

Photos

When Becky shows me a picture of her
and Dan in eighth grade, it is not the Dan
of shaved head and low-slung clothes I know.
This was the Dan of perfect quizzes,
completed homework, the gobbler of science books.
She tells me how they
took the picture on this swing at a dance.
Soon the story is a history with branching roots.

After my mother died, I found a picture
of her and my father with a table of friends.
I told my father everyone looked drunk.
"Only your mother was drunk," he said.
"That's when she drank."
The mother I knew drank one highball at Christmas.
When I told him mother said I was a surprise
because doctors told her no more children,
he insisted I was planned when they could afford me.

My cousin gave me a photo she found
in her mother's drawer, a photo of me
on a dock in an inner tube, an adult bathing cap
swallowing my child head. By the date,
I was five. I cannot recall the place or incident.
My cousin cannot help me find it either;
she was a baby under an oxygen tent at the time.
She owns a companion photo of her mother and mine
swimming near the same dock. The mother I knew
was afraid of water, said she could not swim.
Her mother we never saw in anything but long dark dresses.
Our parents gone now, we can't get back,
can't get a story through anyone's eyes.

Slow Losses

From my father's house,
I watch a man rumble his tractor
across black dirt
while his boy
casts something from behind.

I stare out across land
where bullfrogs once
woke me from sleep,
where crawdads
from the farmer's pond
were easy catch.

Now the farmer's children
sell the land in parcels;
each year subdivisions grow closer,
and motorbikes dig trails in what's left.

Where man and boy now move
within a corridor
of bare March trees,
soon another family
will find some quiet
and worry about the measure of the land.

Neighborhood

Of our first house, only pictures remain.
My baby sitter holding me, we smile
from three wooden steps
where Phyllis poked Frank's eye
with her baton.
In another, my brother
shrugs against a table,
clean as every room is clean
like a tucked fresh sheet.
Mother scooped coal in that basement,
her nightgown hidden by her coat,
while father rewired buildings at night
so the dentist's chair gleamed with light,
and the lawyers' cigar ashes
disappeared with swept shavings.
Now a medical center closes us out
of the block where we ran in tidy yards,
only an easement like a seam
separating one kitchen from another.
The porch where we stuffed grasshoppers
between cracks
is a hospital room now.
On the street where we once belonged,
an IV hangs from its silver pole.

After Signing Releases

The cobalt machine may scare you.
While you wait for the nurse
to speak from another room,
after she lowers your head
like a loaf in a basket,
there are no posters,
no paintings to distract you.
If you close your eyes,
you could be home
vacuuming the rug.
If you can't swallow puree,
tubes keep you from losing weight.
Ice chips cool dry mouth.
When your hair grows back,
the burns may fade,
the inked tattoos might wear off.
Your voice may gargle
like singing into a fan
or puff like air through a straw.
When pain marauds your brain,
the demerol refills.
You can double the dose.
The photograph before treatment
is a record of how you looked.
You will not be radioactive.
Nothing bad is going to happen.

Chemotherapy

Up from bed after three days,
you reach for a curl to twist.
It drops in your hand.
Your other tightens on my arm.
I lean beside you,
rest my cheek next to yours.
We are quiet like the snow outside.
We watch cardinals spill seed from the feeder.
I mention they've lived here a long time;
you tell me you miss the wrens.
I think of when I straddled the chair
to brush the hair I loved to touch,
the hair where I buried my head
to find the familiar curve in your neck.

Today your hair drops
after twenty strokes
into the sack
waiting under the brush.
I rub the smooth pink egg
your head has become,
hold you tight
as you always held me.
Outside it is cold.
We spend the afternoon
combing and recombing a wig,
trying to find the place inside us
where we know this doesn't matter,
waiting to talk until we do.

The Importance of Kneading

She said she'd watched
the seasons change from her recliner,
and this one was her last.
She sat like someone
waiting sleepless in an airport.
I pulled out the bread board,
passed through four mothers,
while she watched icicles
clink on the porch.
"It's my turn now," I told her,
"to learn the secret of bread."
I wanted to learn from her hands
as she did from her mother.
"Don't tell me 'not today.'"
She stared at me for a long time.
"It's all in the kneading," she answered.
"That's all you have to know."

I sifted, warmed yeast with water,
waited in silence with her
while the dough breathed
and seeped over the bowl.
"Punch it down," she spoke,
never having checked a clock.

I buried my hands in the warm mound,
pushed down with the heel of my palm,
over and down, over and down,
until I found the rhythm,
the dough springing back
supple as young skin.

"You'll know by the feel," she called to me.
"Then you'll never forget;
you'll always make good bread."

She scooted on slippers into the kitchen
when I told her I thought it was time,
still not sure what I had to feel.
Her hands sunk in next to mine.
We pushed together
like the times we played duets on the piano.
"There," she said at last,
and I saw in her eyes
what father said was always alive.

Giant Clown

When I called mother
to my bed late at night,
she insisted,
"There's no clown at your window."
His painted frown,
his tapping, gloved hands,
his polka dot tie
haunted my nights
where I tried, under a flood of sweat,
eyes squeezed tight, to lie still
until he went away.

At six, my nephew,
sheet tugged to his eyes,
called me to his bed.
"A giant clown at my window."
"There's no clown,"
I started, then bit those words.
"He's got a rifle and a polka dot tie."
"Where?"
"Right there," he pointed.
"Wanna sleep in my room?" I asked.

When mother started killing cancer pain
with methodone, she was certain
elves built puppets at night across the street,
cows stomped through the house.
"Those things aren't really there,"
I insisted. "It's just the medicine."
One afternoon she added,
"Last night I saw a giant clown
outside the window."
"A clown?" I asked.
"What did he look like?"

Margaret's Song

Once she no longer packed school lunches
or concessioned P. T. A. hot dogs,
she bought the piano
she'd promised herself.
Right off she spilled out *Star Dust*,
her chords thick as custard.
On spring days those chords
crowded the house,
tumbled out windows
through the billowing curtains
of Irma Kidwell's kitchen,
found John Enyeart mulching tomato plants,
reached Jack Lyons turning steaks on the grill,
her hunchbacked fingers
pounding songs she swore no one could write anymore.
Her popular tunes never sounded
quite like melodies anyone hummed,
and she wouldn't play a piece with "too many sharps."
She served *Star Dust* daily like dinner salad,
the last song she played.
In winter her family
gathered around her like a halo,
her chords drowning their "sleep in heavenly peace."
When she refused food
and visitors could come only as close as her music,
she still gave herself to the chords,
to a place even pain couldn't reach.

The Occasional Family

They take a long time climbing stairs,
the black-coated ladies,
their puffy dark hair stiff with hairspray,
their squat, square heels
scooting down aisles.
Their closets full of black dresses,
they are always there
to touch cheeks, to pat hands.
Even if they forget names,
they can link families:
Sam's daughter, Rosie's niece.
They toddle through receiving lines,
scholars at grieving, arms open for the hug;
uncle, third cousin or friend
is always with God at last.
They take close seats to sit it out,
bend fingers in like small cabbages in their laps.
They complain about knees,
touch shoulders in pain,
say they made pignolate or bread all day.
They remember how handsome he used to be,
how hard she always worked.
They sit, cloyed with roses, carnations,
lining the walls on thin wire stands,
dripping over the someone finally at peace
while the men hover in the lobby
like awkward birds.
It's familiar like the carpet
worn more in the center,
the ceiling fans quietly turning,
this accidental, occasional family.

Sisters

She had tea ready when I arrived,
showed me the dress she was fixing,
taking in seams by hand.
"The fabric won't give," she told me.
I handed her the jewelry, my mother's black coat.
She wanted to share her evening bags,
a wedding or dinner party woven into each.
"You can take this one," she offered.
I said no to the evening bag.
"What else can I give you?" she asked
and walked to her curio cabinet
where we touched her figurines.
I lifted the porcelain piece
I've admired for thirty years,
long-necked girl with sloe eyes.
"You like that?" she asked me.
"Then take it. My son won't want it."
We took more tea,
broke shortbread on our plates.
"I have dreams," she told me,
"I talk with my priest.
Before your mother died, I had visions."
I watched her fold her hands, twist in her seat.
"I know I didn't come over enough
when your mother was sick.
Bedre Madre, there was nothing I could do."
I rose to leave, took my plate to the sink,
raised my arms for the usual hug,
but like her fabric, woven too tight,
I couldn't give, I couldn't give.

Wishbone Tradition

The wishes never came true,
but every Christmas
when the turkey was a dinosaurial hull,
and the wishbone had dried in the window,
out came the nutcrackers, nonna's pignolate,
and mother carrying the arched bone.
"Who's gonna wish?" she asked,
looking down at her crew,
languid as arctic seals from father's anisette,
dozing in and out of hearing
how much we needed a white Christmas,
how much wild rice cost this year.
"Needles, pin," she started us out,
"Triplets, twins," father helped.
Sometimes the bone wasn't quite dry,
so greasy it frogkicked through fingers
right on mother's brocade couch.
Some careless years, before father
could wave it like a crackerjack prize,
his grinning face gleaming with turkey scraps,
it broke under his knife.
When we asked why we had to wish,
she pinched fingers together,
punched them in the air.
"You want no cannoli,
no biscotti anymore?
Why you always gotta ask?"
Then she'd give us the look.
It worked on us every year.

The House

I.
Father at the window,
fingers gripping the sill,

eyes sharp on the back fence,
asks if I want the house.

It's a good house, he says,
never looking at me.

Sell it, I say, make
life a smaller parcel.

Too much to move, he answers,
as though time were a short straw.

II.
From the kitchen window
I stare at the yard,

alone with the house
he left behind.

Last spring I cut back
the forsythia without asking,

apologized, sure he would say
I killed it.

He liked the cleared space.
Yellow nubs are ready to open.

III.
The lawyer asks
if I want the house,

says it's best to sell.
I come for mail,

come to check things,
to sit in kitchen sunlight,

to water African violets
I haven't taken home.

Yesterday I packed
a dozen black sacks,

set them by the curb,
one heartload at a time.

Salute

I slit the last bag
of father's crappie,
let the odor sift up
from the sink,
an imprint
of his last summers,
when he sandwiched walking
and meals together
around fishing.
The freezer date,
markered in his even print,
now fading like a watercolor,
was only a month
before my uncle found him--
his face still pink
when I arrived,
no different than Sundays
when he napped,
his flat fingers
interlaced across his chest.
My uncle covered him with a blanket
while I stood waiting
as though any minute
he might open his eyes.
Only hours before
we had tapped wineglasses,
salute,
shared antepasta and linguini,
hugged goodbye before I drove away.
Now I cover the white fillets
with tarragon, lemon, dill,
enough for two to eat.

Tangled with Sleep

Wind in the awnings of another dream?
The lab next door pawing his doghouse?
Someone at your door?
It's the time dreams come unthreaded,
and your father's wave from the garden
drops on the pillow
while you unweave yourself
from sleep.
For a moment the room
is as unfamiliar as a hotel in Madrid.
You wear only the unfinished dream,
spilled out like stolen coins.
It hangs on, piggyback,
like a groggy morning,
walks through the day
inside your footprints.

Winemaking

Rows of stacked crates
bled grape juice
on the basement floor
until the right day, when press spikes
broke through wrinkled skins,
mashed out a flow of juice
flooding across wooden slats
into buckets we carried to barrels
until our soles were suction cups
on a floor scattered with stems.

Uncle and father kept
bottles of their best years
stacked on a shelf
above their barrels.
From first pressing
to final cap,
they savored swigs
until they sampled all.

Later I loaded grapes,
carried buckets
when father inherited the press,
my own barrel beside my brother's,
I went home wrapped in fermented scent,
hair sticky with twigs.

Now my brother packs up
winepress, barrels.
He will take his inheritance home,

try for a good year
with his own sons.
Before packing the shelf,
we swig from a good bottle,
first time without father
who could save it all
if it started to turn,
clear it if it went cloudy,
Salvatore who knew the right day
to bring wine to the family table.

Tuberoses

I. *Family*

Mother sets aside her crocheting,
the afghan a blanket in her lap,
washes cups, leaves the sink clean.
Father finishes his crossword,
rubs his eyes, gives away his yawn.
Before he locks up, he steps outside
to look at stars.
I earmark my chapter,
hear the lock click.
We meet in the hallway to say good night.
The thick scent of tuberoses
slips through our windows.
All night their fragrance
slides within easy dreams.
The attic fan blurs out
the sounds of sleep
one room apart.

II. *After the Funeral*

Dad fidgets in his chair,
alternates his crossword
with turning pages,
stares at crocheted pillows.
He lifts his glasses to yawn.
He talks about fishing, walking.
I sit in mother's chair,
wear her Pendleton jacket,
alternate needlepoint
with staring at her crochet hooks
stacked in their box.
I promise to stay a few days,
get things in order.

We leave the sink clean,
the stove light on as she did,
set anything we move back in its place.
We hug in the hallway.
When he starts the fan,
the scent of her tuberoses
seeps through our windows.
He steps outside to look at stars.

III. *One*

It's been a summer
packing boxes, clearing out
the clothes of the dead,
thumbing through dust
of attic and basement,
transplanting before
father's house sells.
Now in August, beneath my window,
the blooms are out there
on their long thin stalks,
a cluster of trumpets
holding their notes.
A little wind tonight
could nudge them
to blow their scent
across the sill,
perhaps trick my memory
into easy sleep.

Thanksgiving Dinner

While the rolls were rising under the towel,
we nibbled stuffed mushrooms and pickled okra.
String of Pearls floated through the new speakers,
and someone else's mother offered the standby line--
Glenn Miller was music anyone could love.
We toasted the 70 degree day and told stories on each other,
someone always filling the edges of silence.
We browsed through random shots
of one nephew's archaeological summer in Europe
while another tuned in skateboard competitions,
told us John McSomebody invented the sidewall stunt.
My brother and I did not mention mother or father;
we assumed their jobs:
he carved the turkey; I stirred the gravy.
Everyone else discussed the remodeled kitchen,
the pros and cons of wall coverings,
the importance of a good drape.
We passed bowls until our food was cold,
our eyes glassy from wine.
After loading the dishwasher,
we played Michigan Rummy,
where silence was fair game.
We pocketed unspent words,
thought about giving,
played our chips safe.

In Your Own Way

When you show up, Father, it's always with
that smile that had widows bring
casseroles and need new wall switches.
I find you in the faces of white-headed husbands
waiting near dressing rooms, their laps full of sacks.
I smell you still in your hairbrush and bathrobe,
if I plant too deep, hear your voice in the garden.
When I chop garlic, it's your hands at the knife.
As I stare over water, I see you reeling line back,
your cooler full of crappie.
The first time you returned in a dream,
we lounged on lawn chairs in your basement,
drank your best wine.
Gesturing with paddle fingers,
rocking oars in an air sea,
you said I needed a man.
Today, as we watch gulls skim waves,
my husband lounges beside me,
the man you picked in your own way:
as he nods at my gestures,
they are your hands in the air,
your words on my tongue.

Deer Hunting

As soon as we waved away
the last of father's exhaust,
tent and bedroll crowding the back window,
mother called Chicken Delight for delivery,
ready to settle in for the annual weekend
when we did anything we liked.
She was afraid to stay alone, she claimed,
but I always insisted she go first
down the hallway from kitchen to bedrooms
where she switched on lights.
Saturday we lingered in dressing rooms,
traded secrets over lunch.
Dinner was artichoke hearts and black olives
bobbing their silky heads while
we crammed Swiss and salami
between the darkest rye
and crunched fat-fingered dills
still wet from briny crocks.
By eight we watched vampires or werewolves,
sometimes the late show if it starred George Raft.
When we slipped under flowered sheets,
I thought of father, alone with the stars,
the only time quiet was all his,
the only weekend mother was all mine.

The Woodworker
for Lois

For years he retreated
to the workshop under the stairs,
restoring old family rockers,
planing edges of hutch doors,
routing spindles for desk chairs.
Sometimes he planned new pieces,
a bookcase for the library,
a table for the kitchen.

Sometimes she watched
the way he matched and fitted grain,
shaped a little at a time
into a silky finish.
She watched how sandpaper
took the curves of his hand
until heat rose into his palm,
how he brushed away dust,
warmed the color with oils.

When he restored the drop leaf,
she dreamed she woke on his work table,
a rosewood sanded so fine
he could not resist.
Through the steel wool, she felt his joints,
heat rising as he rubbed
her wrinkles into silk.
Her pores drank the oil he offered.
It covered the blush rising in her.

In the Same Place

I miss the man four tables over,
sitting alone, tapping his glass.
I miss the man waiting with notebook
in the class I never took.
I turn too late to the man in the gallery
admiring the same painting,
the man leaving the filling station,
his suit coat over his empty seat.
I miss the man jogging the footpath
an hour before I arrive,
the man four up in the theatre,
three aisles over in the grocery.
I miss the man standing
in his own backyard,
looking at the same April stars,
thinking about the woman
who took the other elevator.
Tonight when we turn alone in our beds,
the invisible one is half asleep on our pillows.
We feel the breath of the other.
For a moment our fingertips touch.

Eating an Artichoke

He selects her from the bin,
the fullest one,
tucks her into his cart
so her green won't bruise.
At home he will rinse and steam her,
soften the stiff leaves,
let the wine breathe.
A little butter brightens her flavor,
a little garlic stuffed inside.
When she seems about ready,
he'll tuck in his napkin,
pour another glass of wine.
The outside limbs go easily;
he scrapes the sparse meat
between his teeth.
Butter gleams down his lip.
He must pry the middle leaves,
tug to free them
for his waiting teeth.
The leaves are softer,
little to discard.
Deep inside, the hairy part.
He scoops this away.
Soon just a moist hollow,
a soft heart.

Replay

Until cousin Sara
sated five lusty smiles,
a knife gouged
between her legs,

Emily had forgotten
the hairy legs,
her knees pinned wide.

Now that blind date
reels behind Emily's eyelids
like too many drinks.
Sundress ripped open,
sundress ripped open,
the reel replays.

When she grabs the quilt,
he unwinds her,
a bare spool
spinning into the hallway,
where no doors unlatch.

Rug-burned,
she grabs doorknobs,
kicks over chairs.
He grinds knees into hers,
says, "enjoy it,"
before the pillow
sucks up her scream.

He shoves.
He shoves.
The reel replays.

The last is hers,
a shove that knocks him
against the mirrored wall,
a hundred hairy legs
falling on the rug,
a hundred hairy legs.

Forsythia

The forsythia, a wall of tangles
in the back yard,
was privacy —
until I flushed out children
who built summer forts,
rabbits who lowered the parsley.
The clipping and bundling,
the itch of poison ivy,
the sting of wild thorns:
not worth
the space it covered.
I hacked it down,
hoping to start over, keep it spare.
But it was back in a season
like our recurring arguments.
Helping me,
my neighbor sliced through trunks
and sprayed remaining stubs.
We bundled and raked
until dusk closed in
like a slow answer.
Two shadows packed his truck,
then the branches passed out of sight
like the glow of a taillight
in the rain.
Nothing left to keep up —
nothing but chemicals, nettles.
It would take time,
time to pull loose.

Arguments

Like gutter leaves,
words clog the flow.
They spew from plunged drains
months of black sludge.

Like spinning blades,
words surprise us, like traps,
confuse us, change us.

Some pop out
like the wrong lead
in bridge,
the chess move
we want back.

Words are hibernating fleas,
fossils left behind.
Shadows follow words, hang around.
We're always looking back.

Anne's Pond

A skink's neon stripes
flicker in the sun
like old movies
in a dark theatre.
Masked waxwings
bob and dip
on thin branches
hanging over the clog
in the stream
where water doesn't
carry anything but
wears a leaf-cluttered veil,
a hairnet holding in place
what needs to go.

Birds Along the Highway

They gather
liked ticketed passengers
arranging themselves
against the falling sun
like a flurry of buckshot,
a scatter of tiny planes
signaling to rise
from the dry leaves
and fly
through the splinters
of sunlight,
working out the pattern
as they go.

A Chance to Talk

When you suggested a walk on your father's farm,
I pictured bullfrogs and reeds,
a blanket laid with bread and Brie,
but you stomped us across acres
of soybeans, a sea of waving stalks
snapping off brown dust as we elbowed through.
Your rifle ready to pick off squirrels,
you taunted I probably objected to guns,
thought animals should all be pets.
Behind you I gasped, your words blowing
by with the wind. As comfortable as a
snowsuited toddler suddenly down in a drift,
I didn't say you walked too fast,
didn't ask why you never looked back.
Behind you my hiking boots gathered mud,
slabs I dragged along.
My sweater wore a shield of sticktights,
my hair spears of dry weeds.
While you bobbed like a buoy farther ahead,
I fought the waves of soybeans nudging me back.
Jetsam on your heavy boat,
I slipped below your sea.

Minnows

A phone call for news,
a ride in his new Porsche,
dinner when he gets a raise--
enough to bait thoughts.
He tosses you a minnow,
nothing more.

A thousand minnows form phosphorescent walls,
enough light to see by
while gliding, weightless
through salt water.
Swimming through them
disperses
a thousand silver flashes.

Out of water, a minnow flaps,
too slippery in a palm.
Its silver
is small, fast,
one shine, then gone.

Just a Little Thought

Under the bed, behind the unused blanket,
the center too thin for winter nights,
I found your letters.
I unfolded one, unopened a dozen years.
It was cold in Ohio,
snow collected on your window ledge.
You held up the ivy plant
with colored pencils, counted new leaves.
It was always cold in Ohio,
except the summer we learned tennis,
played gin rummy for dares.
We were content then
with shaking pudding in a jar,
making brownies in a skillet.
When you finally came home,
promises broke sudden as glasses
you hurled against the wall.
Empty bottles explained your red eyes.
I took the key back; you took the rum.
Your smell hung in the closet, on the pillows.
For a long time phone calls
hustled me from sleep.
Even when you smashed the glass door,
I didn't let you in.
Those stones inside me are finally
as cold as Ohio,
and you're just a little thought,
a worn thread under a nail.

On Grand Cayman

for Greg

We pass a seafan between us,
bend to wash sand from a conch.
Below the water, we point at squirrel fish,
dodge fire coral,
our legs and hands grazing
as we slip, horizontal,
through clear water.

With ease we groom each other:
I dab your razor cuts,
you wipe lipstick from my teeth,
pull sand burrs from my heel.
When your back aches,
I rub the knot.

We are good at only touching,
at sharing cereal from the same box,
our clothes in the same wash,
at halfing our mangoes, our Key Lime pie.

The moon rises above us,
washes the white beach
with enough light to walk,
one on sand,
one in the sea.

On the line, we hang wet suits together,
let the wind fill them
with our invisible shapes.
Inside we turn,
half awake, half asleep.

What We Become

Crabs sink into holes when approached,
clatter like wind snagged in dry leaves.
Not wanting to leave the island
or who we become here,
we take the ocean's voice inside us
as seashells that still sing
miles from the nudge of waves.
We slip out past where waves
rocked us against coral,
past water safe and shallow.
Beyond the reef wall,
sting rays glide above us
like flat black stars.
I scatter a wall of minnows,
their silver splitting like moonlight,
find you on the other side.
We plunge deeper together
in long, lazy loops,
until we are one circle,
spinning and turning into itself.

I Dream of the Wrong Men
Days Before the Wedding

In the darkest part of sleep they come,
one each night to say goodbye.
The dark one brings fresh salmon and coffee beans,
Cyrano's silent tears. He mostly nods.
The silver-haired one is no more than a mist,
a fog that comforts yet blinds.
Inside his velvet sack is a knife.
The diver brings a seahorse he's tamed,
the nature lover some fresh viola, already wilting.
Some offer last kisses, brush fingertips as they leave.
The angry one stays huddled against the wind,
leaning into a tree with his bottle and a poem.
They each linger with a last expression,
their final gift trapped as in amber resin.
In the last dream they line up together,
pilgrims carrying light over a hill.
When I unravel from sleep,
against the cold pane,
I press my forehead,
cup my eyebrow to check the horizon.

Mated

All night they turn,
one toe or fingertip
hanging on to the other.
Never quite lost
in the shifting waves of sleep,
their dreams cross over
into each other's.
Early splinters of light
divide one rooted shadow
into two.
They nuzzle closer
before either knows why.
Light takes the shadow
balanced on her shoulder,
another down his long back.
They inch back in parts,
their roots deeper
than the speech of morning.

Composition

1
As you wave from the sailboat,
I move you into the lower third
of the lens, include the red flag,
day's taillight on the sea.

2
You carry words you've collected
into paragraphs, stanzas,
offer them like fresh peaches,
like a passel of prayers.

3
Before dinner we arrange verticals of
dried eucalyptus, bamboo, prairie grasses.
A curled reed crosses the vase rim,
points at dusk, disappearing behind trees.

4
In the kitchen I stir walnuts into dough,
arrange black olives, red pepper strips
on a bed of romaine,
add a lemon slice.

5

Near your easel you arrange a pear,
a long-necked bottle, a wine glass
on a tablecloth, then mix greens
on your palette.

6

Upstairs grandmother needlepoints
beside fresh-cut bluebells,
motionless below lamplight.

7

Stretched out on floor pillows,
we listen to Corelli,
read passages from Neruda
while gardenias release their scent.

8

When your arm encloses me,
I lean into your curves.
We are colored oils
swirling on a skin of water.

Mask Making
in a Farmhouse Kitchen

Clustered, we waited
for wet plaster strips
to cover vaselined faces
until we were voiceless,
trapped in a facial moment
we might never pose again,
incubating, somewhere
where there were no faces,
until cool fingers
lifted away a shell of ourselves.

We set white faces
to harden in the sun,
faces that drew us back
to stare, to touch
the hard, white cheek.

When we tried them on,
one said the early people of Jericho
called them death masks,
spirits trapped in faces.
Another said artists
call them life masks,
faces exact images.
At home, I hang mine
in the window.
Against morning backlight,
it stares back at me,
a stranger
from every angle,
a hidden self,
even when I try it on.

Saying Goodbye to the Children

It's begun again, soundless,
but not without fanfare,
blood leaking through me,
through my skirt,
my own broken oil seal.
Clots unfold like carnival flowers
blooming in the white water bowl,
red strings twisting into familiar shapes.
My body's saying it's not too late.
For months it's been like this,
these sudden surges soaking
cotton tubes I drop in the basket,
my body taking over without me.
And the blood comes more often,
hanging on longer,
precursor to paucity,
monsoons before dunes.
Each time I say goodbye to the children,
linked to life by only a thought,
the misshapen, voiceless flowers
sinking and blooming below water,
waving back, waving goodbye.

About to Get Up

Thick flakes spin
around the streetlight.
A couple across the street,
their engine flooded,
begin a snowball fight.
Their voices rise above white breath.
She sidewinds up the yard,
his snowball scattered in her hair.
When he catches her,
they tumble in the snow.
I am watching an old memory.
I know the next part.
He dusts snow from her hair,
cups her chin.
They disappear into their Volkswagon igloo.
Snowflakes clump on awnings;
they still don't drive away.
I still don't move.
I'd like to catch
snowflakes in my mouth,
have someone cup my face
in his hands.
I tell myself it's too cold.
My body is its own heavy clump.
The furnace offers a rumble
like a car about to turn over,
like a person about to get up.

Pilgrims

Along this path, it's easier
to hunt bittersweet than meaning.
Afternoon sunlight haloes milkweed
tangled in thorns,
silhouettes spiky heads
of Queen Anne's lace
cocked upward
as if sure of the unknown
like pilgrims:
still and still moving.
Along this trail we hike
where bluffs hide us
when we rest.

What we shall do
has not yet come to light;
we are still on our way.

Women's Work

for Louise

She needlepointed rows of
wool stitches,
as we sat through
committee meetings,
the rest of us
waving and shouting.
Years later I learned
the calm of needlework from her.
Once we spent a morning
planning projects,
sorting skeins of unused yarn,
lost in combinations:
teal with peach and ivory,
burgundy with taupe or cream.
When her husband barbed
about excess yarn,
I remembered father
trying to argue about shirts
mother gave to Goodwill.
"This is your baptism dress,"
she said, ignoring him
as we sorted through trunks.
"And this was your birthday dress at two."
Like her, Louise went on about pine with gray
and wasn't the yellow nice with navy.

Cafeteria Lady

Her hairnet, a spiderweb
above her eyebrows,
her white uniform
speckled with cinnamon,
her buttons stretched tight
in torn holes,
not once does she
speak or smile as
we scoot our trays
down silver rails.
She scoops stewed fruit
or runny cobbler,
gazes past us
through a window
opened to a world
we cannot see.

Orange: The Color of Abundance

On public radio, Russell Somebody announced
he grew a 570-pound pumpkin.
I wondered why, knowing summers we planted seeds
pumpkins strangled cucumbers, crossbred with squash,
until we donated to the boy scouts
the orange bumps peeking up in moonlight.
For years they volunteered through spring dirt.

Russell Somebody sold his hybrid seeds
to Somebody Sawyer who grew a 620-pound pumpkin.
Russell said a pumpkin that big
you can watch grow inches every day.
I thought pumpkin tarts, cookies,
cakes for Ethiopia,
pies for Boys Town,
bread for the Presbyterian fund raiser,
soup for the mission of mercy.
While he talked about setting records,
I wondered what was Russell Somebody
going to do with his pumpkin.

Snow Angels

for Ann and David

We stomp boot tracks
under a bleached sky.
Our cold smoke breath
is an aura around our
caps and ski jackets.
Winter has left seamed scars
in its drifts, arched high
like a cat's stretch.
We will make snow angels
near the lagoon,
where last spring,
we drank Chablis from plastic cups.
When we climb the hill,
we look back
at the white-winged bodies,
wondering how long before
we can't find them again.
We follow our boot prints back
as if we know where we're going.

Convergence

This morning the choir in church
booms out so loud
even I sing full,
not hiding words in my throat.
I hear my notes,
some of them in tune.
The lady in front of me
enters on the third bar,
some notes snagging in her throat,
her eyes startled as a fledgling.
The woman, always in a hat,
raises her hymnal higher.
A grey suit, lifesavers
usually on his tongue,
chews a little O to sing.
We are all there.
The church fills
with the crossing of voices,
filling the space
where things sometimes converge.

Scraps

"For me, writing is assembling," Juneil says,
leaning into the porch sun,
her chin resting on a thumb.
"I write lines at work on scraps of paper
when no one's looking.
At night I lay them out to see order,
to find what goes where."
"You should write about that," I tell her,
imagining scraps in drawers or pockets,
Juneil at her desk moving around moments,
trying to bring sense to so many scraps.
I think of my own scraps, how smart Juneil is
to piece together what I leave unraveled.
"You write the poem," she smiles.
"I just assemble."

Photograph

I took it from the attic suitcase
of nonna's snapshots,
a black and white past
of cross-armed uncles leaning against roadsters,
cousins sucking in pasta,
bisnonna in the fields of Bivona,
papa laying peonies over gravestones--
faces before I was born.
In this shot, nonna stands beside a Pieta,
one hand clutching an alligator bag,
one hand over her heart,
alone with God at Capistrano.
When I stayed with her,
she clicked rosary beads,
eyes half mast, silk stockings rolled to ankles,
her lips shaping words she never shared.
After she knelt for prayers at bedtime,
she turned down our blankets,
said good night to nonno,
who slept in his own bed,
then climbed between satin sheets,
alone, as she always was with God.

Islanders at Cayman Kai

They are silhouettes,
their boat anchored
at the shore of the reef.
The father, thigh-deep in water,
his shirt flapping against dark skin,
casts a line with only his hands.
His son leans back in the boat,
cups his eyes seaward, soon launched
by rhythms of water and waiting.
When something drags on his hands,
the father pulls his line in.
His son, bent and lean as a staple,
applauds as his father
loops slack over shoulder
and backs up against coral.
The algae slick, he dips down, up,
a feint with balance,
while the line tugs and plunges,
back toward the sea.
His hold is solid;
he wraps his line with a wrist,
his son waving their net like a flag.
A barracuda slices forward in the wave.
One final jerk sends him surging,
chin-sliding into white sand.
He flips, kicks his tail
in useless figure eights
while his gills pulse and fall.

Dream of Finding Treasure

Home from Grand Cayman,
we are brown as seabeans,
water-worn as Blackbeard's treasure
hidden somewhere in a cave we never found.
My brother greets us
wearing spandex and sneakers,
a whistle around his neck,
an oat bran bar in his pocket.
He is smiling as though he is not
about to lose his house, his marriage.
He is sweaty as though he's
actually been exercising, has
even lost his sixty-pound middle,
his need always to sit down.
I ask for the mail he's collected.
He shows me catalogues.
I ask about bills.
He tells me mother paid them
along with his mortgage.
I tell him mother's
been dead seven years.
He says she found him a job.
I walk into the kitchen,
see my face in the stove,
scrubbed to the shine mother
demanded of hers.
I stare out into July darkness,
the driveway covered with snow,
the street a long black fissure
choking with gold doubloons.

The Fisherman Rebaits His Line

"That's the reason they're called lessons...
because they lessen from day to day."

for Robert Bly

We were six walking the coast,
some ankle deep in water.
We came upon a fisherman,
his bucket full of flounder,
his long pole a siphon to the sea.
Our teacher borrowed a fish,
set it on the beach
and instructed us to watch.
It arched and rocked
its flat-disked body,
its blue dots disappearing.
Sand gritted its gills
as they opened and closed.
We turned away, then back
to stare at what would linger
with its own afterlife
like odors in sea sponges
or the ocean rush in conch shells.
When the flounder was still,
the fisherman flopped him
back in his carrying bucket,
rebaited his line and waited,
as he did for other flounder
he'd hooked from the sea,
and we walked on down the beach,
shoulders brushing,
our silence a tuning fork
fading from wave to wave.